Shrike Shrublands

Steve Jones

Published by Steve Jones, 2023.

Also by Steve Jones

Shrike Shrublands
Wildlife Watching Around Ventnor, Isle of Wight
Writers in the Wild

Watch for more at Stevecjones.uk.

Table of Contents

1 Introduction 1
1.1 Why do we need Shrike Shrublands? 5
1.2 What makes a high-quality Shrike Shrubland? 6
1.3 Biodiversity values 11
1.4 Woodland creation as an unmet opportunity 15
1.5 High nature value farming or rewilding? 17
1.6 Long-term development 18
2. Creating Shrike Shrublands 19
2.1 Selecting a site 20
2.2 Starting land use 23
2.3 Some early interventions 25
3 Three stylised examples 38
3.1 Arable field on chalk 39
3.2 Improved pasture and amenity grassland 42
3.3 Woodlands edge 45
4. Managing Shrike Shrublands 48
5. Discussion and conclusions 51
6. Further reading 52
7. Acknowledgements 53
8. About the author 54

Dedicated to all those promoting natural regeneration as the best way to create new woodlands and open grassy-shrubland habitats! With your efforts, we may see the recovery of our Turtle Dove, Nightingale, Whinchat and Dormouse populations and, perhaps, the return of the Butcher Bird, to the British countryside.

If you enjoy reading this guide please consider leaving a review on your online bookshop of choice. This helps other people find it. Thank you.

1 Introduction

'Scrub' is a much-maligned habitat in official UK conservation and farming circles. Scrub 'invades' other habitats. Volunteers conduct 'scrub bashing' weekends. Farmers can lose public payments if there's 'too much' scrub in their pasture.

Of course, the colonisation of important old grasslands by shrubs and trees can be enormously damaging to their existing values if left unchecked. But very often valuable areas of scrub are removed without good cause. I recently observed as a local Wildlife Trust systematically removed small, scattered patches of Dogwood, Wayfaring Tree and Elder from otherwise very open chalk grassland on the orders of the statutory conservation agency, removing long-standing features and reducing habitat heterogeneity to no good effect.

Grassland-shrub mosaics can be enormously valuable, dynamic habitats. Yet we seem to resent their very existence and miss numerous opportunities to create more of them. A baffling example of this: many of our most prominent, respected, and influential nature conservation organisations choose to bypass the early successional stage of grassland-with-scattered-shrubs-and-trees in woodland creation projects. They instal solid plantations of even-aged whips (nursery transplants of trees and shrubs), bypassing the wonderfully biodiverse grassland-shrub mosaic stage of ecological succession that, under nature-guided circumstances, would be a normal part of woodland community assembly. I'm not suggesting that such dense planting isn't appropriate in some circumstances. I've done some myself. What I *am* suggesting is that extensive planting should not be the *default approach* to woodland creation where significant nature conservation gain is the objective.

The gradual, sequential, unpredictable colonisation of open areas by trees, shrubs and herbaceous plants is a fascinating and enormously important part of nature recovery. The natural process of species assembly itself is an attribute of biodiversity that should be valued.

In woodland creation projects, rather than planting wall-to-wall thickets of even-age whips, we should always consider aiming early on for a *mosaic* of species-rich scrub and locally disturbed, structurally complex, species-rich grassland with enormous value for wildlife, including many species of conservation concern.

As these grassland-shrubland mosaics develop they can give additional positive benefits: they can gradually absorb atmospheric carbon; attenuate rainfall and reduce water run-off owing to their roughness and gluey organic matter build-up; provide wonderful spreading space for people; provide high-quality, healthy grazing and browsing habitat for livestock and space for the conservation of rare livestock breeds; and, of course, be a cost-effective precursor to natural woodland and wood pasture development.

It's time we ditched the derogatory 'scrub' label and championed species-rich grassy 'shrublands'.

This short booklet seeks to encourage the creation of new species-rich grassland-shrubland mosaics - 'Shrike Shrublands' - **on existing species-poor sites**, such as hitherto intensively managed pasture and arable land, and amenity grassland.

The words 'scrub' and 'scrubland' are here replaced by the words 'shrub' and 'shrubland' to signify a more positive stance. I hope the term 'grassy shrubland' creates an image for you of a mosaic of grassland with scattered shrubs, rather than a thicket of shrubs. The latter is valuable but here we include the ever-so-vital flowering grassland element.

Why '*Shrike*' Shrubland? A couple of years ago I was asked to investigate prospects for the return of the Red-backed Shrike to southern England. During that investigation for the RSPB and the Knepp Estate in Sussex, I came across a 2002 paper by Dr Andy Evans and Des Vanhinsbergh (*Habitat associations of the Red-backed Shrike (Lanius collurio) in Carinthia, Austria*). In one part of that and a related paper the authors set out how one might create perfect habitat for Red-backed Shrikes. What was immediately clear was that perfect Red-backed Shrike habitat is one that contains a rich community of species associated with dynamic, open, often early successional habitats, and some of those characteristic species are of conservation concern here in the UK and across north-west Europe.

Their paper and my visits to the Knepp Estate inspired this booklet.

The Red-backed Shrike - the Butcher Bird - was once a widespread species across our countryside but is now effectively extinct in the UK as part of our summer breeding avifauna.

After their demise as a regular breeding species here, and a protracted decline in north-west Europe, prospects for a return to the UK of the Butcher Bird have seemed remote. But with very recent hints of recovery on the near-continent in response to habitat creation by farmers and a couple of favourable summers, we might just entice Red-backed Shrikes back if we create lots of favourable habitat for them.

So, if we can create new Shrike Shrublands scattered across the UK, we might just see the return of the Butcher Bird.

The perfect territory for a Shrike is good for such an enormous variety of species that creating this habitat should be enthusiastically encouraged regardless. This is truly a straightforward and 'no regrets' investment and the creation of Shrike Shrublands should be a central pillar of nature recovery across farmland.

This short book aims to advocate for this habitat and to give an overview of how to go about creating it.

1.1 Why do we need Shrike Shrublands?

The Red-backed Shrike is a wonderful ambassador species for a neglected habitat - open, sunny, species-rich grassland-shrubland mosaics.

Breeding Red-backed Shrikes have a specific set of requirements from a high-quality territory. If we can create blocks of habitat, each capable of satisfying a few pairs of nesting Red-backed Shrikes, we can be sure that it will be bustling with wildlife, including some other priority species of conservation concern.

1.2 What makes a high-quality Shrike Shrubland?

To paint a picture of the perfect Shrike Shrubland, let's describe the perfect Red-backed Shrike territory, then scale up so the shrubland can support a few pairs of Shrikes. Bigness is beautiful.

A high-quality Shrike Shrubland is comprised of *widely spaced* clumps of native, often thorny, shrubs - Field and Dog Rose, Bramble, Hawthorn, Blackthorn, Elder, Crab Apple - with the occasional taller shrub and emergent tree, distributed across a mosaic of very short-grazed lawns with scattered patches of disturbed ground, and areas of taller, flower-rich grassland.

Crucially, *large* invertebrates - beetles, bumblebees, grasshoppers and crickets, and dragonflies - are abundant. Larger members of those insect groups are among the main prey items of Red-backed Shrikes, including their broods and fledgelings.

An extensive thicket of shrubs lacking open ground is generally much less valuable and would be largely avoided by shrikes.

The Red-backed Shrike is a sit-and-scan hunter. They love to perch out on the strands of shrubs in open grassland, waiting for potential prey to come into view.

The hunting shrike really loves an unimpeded view. The thin strand of a Field Rose branch extending up above a small mound of bramble is the perfect vantage point, as is a fence post within or strand of wire crossing open, species-rich grassland.

It's mostly looking for beetles scurrying across the ground and bumblebees visiting herbaceous wildflowers. As soon as it sees a large invertebrate it flies quickly towards it and catches it, either on the ground if it's a beetle or grasshopper, or in the air if it's a flower-visiting bumblebee or hunting dragonfly.

It will then fly back to its perch or another one nearby to devour its prey. It will often skewer prey on a favoured barb or spine. Or, if there's a nest nearby, it'll take the food straight to the nest to provision its brood.

Shrikes have an inordinate fondness for larger beetles. They capture these on the ground. Favourite beetles include those associated with animal dung. Beetles using cattle dung seem to be particularly popular. There would have been plenty of dung when Bison and Aurochs herds roamed wild European shrublands. The dung of domestic livestock once supported these dung associated invertebrates too, but the prophylactic use of anti-parasitic Avermectin drugs has had a dramatic, deleterious impact on invertebrates shrikes depend on to raise their broods, so it's essential that such chemicals aren't present in the dung of animals grazing Shrike Shrublands.

Shrikes want their food to be easily accessible. For beetles captured on the ground, this means they want to be able to scan across nearby lawns of tightly grazed sward and areas of churned up ground. So tightly grazed lawns directly below and around isolated clumps of shrubs, say Bramble, Dog and Field Rose, and Hawthorne, are ideal.

But the beetles are scurrying between tussocky grassland or piles of dung, or, for some species, animal carcasses. So, for both the beetles and the Shrikes, we need an intricate mosaic of lawns and taller, rougher grassland with a bit of very light summer grazing, to provide the dung.

The bumblebees, also crucial for Shrikes feeding their offspring, need copious quantities of nectar-rich wildflowers from early spring throughout the summer into late autumn. Both the shorter lawns and the areas of taller, more tussocky grassland should thus be a mass of flowering herbaceous plants from early spring to late autumn.

Bumblebees and other nectar seeking invertebrates love sheltered, sunny swards. The microclimates created by an intricately varied landform and scattered stands of shrubs are perfect. Streams and clean water pools within and close to the shrubland will draw in dragonflies and damselflies.

That's the basic ingredients of a good Red-backed Shrike territory. Now scale up and imagine a patch of that habitat capable of supporting a few territories side-by-side. That's a Shrike Shrubland.

Although the Red-backed Shrike is essentially extinct as a regular breeding species in the UK, climatic conditions for it are widely suitable here and are projected to become more favourable for them through time due to anthropogenic climate change.

But Red-backed Shrikes will not track their climate space unless they're doing well on the near-continent and habitat is available here in the UK. If their populations on the near continent increase, and they come to saturate habitat there, migrant shrikes may increasingly spill into the UK each spring. Creating Shrike Shrublands along the lines outlined in this short book will do a lot to welcome shrikes should they be in a position to attempt to recolonise.

But providing this habitat is about much more than just providing a welcoming habitat for any shrikes seeking to establish territories. It's about creating blocks of habitat that will support an array of wildlife.

Some key elements of a wildflower-rich shrubland

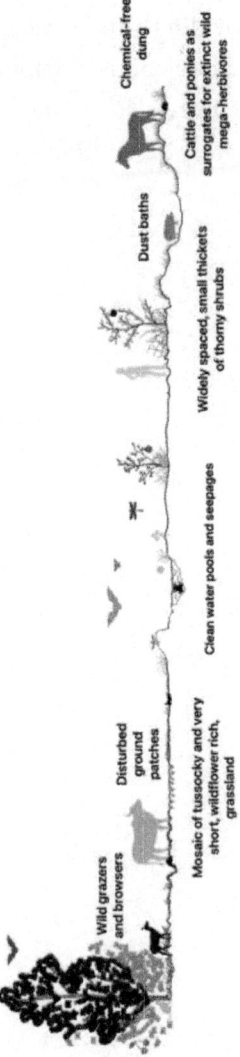

1.3 Biodiversity values

A shrubland-grassland mosaic with the various attributes outlined in this guide will be capable of supporting a high abundance of plants and animals and a richness of species. In the early years it will likely support many species characteristic of early successional habitat. Over time, species associated with older habitat features will likely appear. If the site initially lacks old trees with rot holes, for example, species associated with such micro-habitats will only start to appear after many decades. Greater complexity needs time to develop.

In this section, I'll very briefly highlight a few species that may well come to use created, open Shrike Shrublands in the early years. For a thorough deep dive, read the free JNCC report, *The Nature Conservation Value of Scrub*, a copy of which can be found via the link provided at the end of this booklet.

First, a shrubland of the sort described here will support many flowering herbaceous wildflower species. This community will be dominated by hitherto commonplace wildflowers that once graced most or all farmed grasslands. Species present within a given site will vary depending on conditions at a very small scale: tall areas of grassland will contain some species not present in more tightly grazed lawns; wet flushes will support wetland loving species; dry, summer parched areas will support species adapted to drought. Disturbed ground will support yet a different set of species. This kind of complexity of conditions brings with it diversity and richness.

A richness of flowering species will ensure there's nectar and pollen available from very early spring through summer and into the late autumn. Some wildflowers will even bloom through the winter. These need not be rare species. Just a rich assemblage of common wildflowers.

An extended flowering season is vital to the lives of many dependent invertebrates. Different species of bumblebee for example have different flight periods during the year. Whatever the species, and whenever they're on the wing, they need lots of wildflowers to provide nectar for fuel.

Abundant flowering species helps support rich invertebrate communities. Again, these will be overwhelmingly common and widespread species. Many of them will have declined greatly in abundance in recent decades. Because there's a mosaic of both taller grassland, and very short grazed lawns, bumblebees will find abundant nest building opportunities. Common grasshoppers will also be very much at home in this intricate mosaic of sward heights and structures.

Animal dung will be a frequent and ever-present resource scattered widely. Because this is free of toxic anti-parasitic chemicals, it will provide vital food resources for various invertebrates, including beetles favoured by shrikes.

The edges of scattered shrub mounds will likely provide sheltered basking spots for reptiles such as Common Lizard and Adder. Bush crickets will thrive here too.

Common bats of various species will find plenty of food over a Shrike Shrubland. Some scarcer species may utilise the site if they're in the area.

Several notable birds of conservation concern may well breed within Shrike Shrublands depending on their location, context and habitats within and around them. Turtle Doves, for example, may nest within thicker shrub patches, especially if there are clean water pools and annual seed-rich habitat within the shrubland or close by. Shrublands positioned within mixed, wildlife friendly farmland with arable is probably best for them, if the arable includes spring cereals and areas of fallow through the summer. Linnets are also an obligate seed-eater and will be present year-round. They tend to nest in small colonies within pockets of shrubs distributed across open grassland. Patches of Bramble and Gorse embedded within a grassy shrubland will more than likely support a colony of Linnets.

Nightingales may well colonise, but their tastes are not yet fully understood. They're to some extent a species of early successional habitats, perhaps where they're somewhat moist rather than summer parched.

Open shrubby habitat of this nature supports Dormouse on the Isle of Wight and in parts of Dorset. Hedgehogs will probably much appreciate a shrubland if they are present in the area.

Cirl Buntings are currently restricted to the south-west of England. But the population has increased dramatically over the last two decades due to concerted conservation efforts. They may well expand along the south coast east into Dorset and Hampshire. A Shrike Shrubland is likely to come into its own as a grasshopper-rich summer nesting habitat for Cirl Buntings if there's sufficient annual seed-rich habitat nearby support them over winter. Although the all-important disturbed soil patches within a Shrike Shrubland will support broadleaved annual wildflowers, a source of seeds needed by Cirl Buntings through the winter, these alone will probably not be enough to see the buntings through the late winter and early spring 'hungry gap' when weed seeds have been depleted by hungry beaks and invertebrates are scarce.

Blocks of Shrike Shrublands, as well as hedgerow systems, interspersed within arable with some spring cereal cropping are likely to be needed to support Cirl Buntings (and Turtle Doves).

Yellowhammers seem to range more widely than Cirl Bunting and remain widespread if no longer common. This is the most likely bunting to utilise Shrike Shrublands for nesting in summer in regions with mixed farming.

If your site is close to or contains within it wetlands, dragonflies and damselflies will likely be common. In late summer and autumn hunting dragonflies can be especially abundant in this kind of habitat.

It's important to note that the account above addresses the early years of a shrubland. Those sorts of results and values will persist if your shrubland is managed in the long-term to maintain an open grassland-shrub mosaic. But if your longer-term aim is to develop woodland, there will be a fascinating and natural turnover of species, with open habitat specialists tending to be replaced by those of cooler, more shady woodland habitats, including an array of scarce species. This will take many decades to unfold.

1.4 Woodland creation as an unmet opportunity

Native woodland creation is a high priority in the UK, and this priority offers an exciting route to create a shifting mosaic of Shrike Shrublands across whole landscapes and regions. To meet this opportunity, Shrike Shrubland creation could come to largely replace the common practice of wall-to-wall planting of nursery tree and shrub transplants (whips). Dense planting of whips usually rapidly bypasses open, sunny, early successional mosaics of seedling trees, shrubs and grassland advocated in this booklet.

Dense planting is partly designed to address often high mortality rates of whips. But it also leads very rapidly to a continuous, low, closed thicket across the whole planted area. This is entirely unsuitable for nesting Red-backed Shrikes and many of the other species associated with its habitat.

In the context of new native woodland creation, Shrike Shrublands can be a temporary phase in the gradual development of closed canopy woodland or more open wood pasture.

If most, or at least many, current native woodland creation projects opted for assisted natural regeneration, to plant trees and shrubs as *scattered clumps* in open grassland or on arable, rather than for extensive planting of wall-to-wall whips, we would see a shifting mosaic of open Shrike Shrublands initiated across our countryside. As advocated here, efforts would be made to enhance the wildflower richness and density within the open grassland component, too, recognising that this will ultimately be replaced by species favouring more shady conditions.

Numerous new grassland-shrublands could be created annually; we'd have every successional stage represented numerous times and ever-changing wildlife communities associated with each.

Where the long-term intention at a particular site is to retain a more open flowering grassland with scattered small thickets of shrubs, appropriate management can be used to maintain a more permanent, but dynamic, open habitat.

1.5 High nature value farming or rewilding?

Anyone can create a Shrike Shrubland. Not so long ago species-rich grasslands with scattered shrub clumps, as well as wood pasture, were characteristic of our farmed landscapes. Shrubland-grassland mosaics would certainly fit in very well with regenerative and other forms of high nature value farming and provide excellent space for rare livestock breeds, many of which are mixed feeders (enjoying both shrubs and herbaceous vegetation.)

Although the British Isles were extensively wooded, more open mosaics of species-rich grassland and scattered shrubs and trees were also a natural, pre-agricultural feature of the British countryside, just the sort of habitat likely loved by Aurochs and Bison across large parts of Europe. So the creation of Shrike Shrublands can also be an example of active rewilding.

Shrike Shrubland creation is for everyone. Every farmer and landowner across the country, whether they consider themselves to be a high nature value farmer, a rewilder, or a bit of both can create this wonderful habitat.

1.6 Long-term development

Suppose you have a plot of, say, five acres you'd like to turn into a Shrike Shrubland. In your mind's eye, how do you expect your shrubland to look in 20, 50, 100 years' time? Are you looking to stand back and just allow it to develop under its own steam? Are you specifically looking to create an area of high-quality natural woodland? Perhaps you envisage wood pasture, with grazing livestock or wild herbivores, or both. Or perhaps you'd like to maintain an open, dynamic mosaic of shrubs and grassland for the long-term?

Your choices will determine how to treat the site in the decades to come, but a Shrike Shrubland can and should be a prelude to all those trajectories. We'll consider your longer-term aspirations at points in the following two sections, addressing shrubland creation, and long-term management.

2. Creating Shrike Shrublands

In this section of the guide we'll first discuss some generic components that are likely to be present within most or all high-quality Shrike Shrublands. We'll then briefly outline how one might integrate these various generic components within three stylised contexts: arable reversion, open improved grassland, and woodland edge.

2.1 Selecting a site

Size and shape: This booklet deals with larger blocks of habitat rather than linear hedgerows with margins. The latter, without doubt, can be enormously valuable for wildlife within farmland. Hedgerows and flower-rich margins distributed within high nature value farmland, with, for example, species-rich grasslands and low-intensity arable, will be very important for wildlife.

There is a good collection of books setting out how to manage linear hedgerows, field margins and similar features.

Here, we deal with larger, round or rectangular blocks of habitat.

By larger blocks, we mean areas of several acres or hectares to tens or even hundreds of acres or hectares. The larger the better. If you have, say, a five acre arable field or paddock, that would make a superb shrubland for a pair or two of shrikes. As the size of the area in question increases, so too does its biodiversity potential.

Bigger sites have more deep interior, less influenced by what's going on at the immediate margins, and can support larger, and perhaps denser, populations of various species. They can also embrace a broader range of conditions such as soil moisture gradients and topography, boosting species richness.

If you intend to allow cattle to graze your shrubland, and this is certainly recommended if the dung is free of antiparasitic chemicals, then embedding the site within a much larger grazing unit could work very well. Hemming any livestock into a relatively small site, especially in summer, will substantially reduce its value. If cattle can range across a much larger area and only visit the Shrike Shrubland every few days, say, or as just occasional animals, this will help to ensure flowering plants can bloom abundantly and that a mosaic of herbaceous vegetation will be maintained throughout the summer.

Consider wild fire risk: In their early stages of development, areas of open grassland and scattered shrubs can be vulnerable to wildfire. In time, they may become less vulnerable.

Some attributes of the habitat described below may reduce fire risk. For example, reinstating seepages and creating networks of pools can provide effective breaks to grass fires. Lawns of tightly grazed sward and disturbed ground breaking up more tussocky grassland can also be effective firebreaks. Avoiding very large blocks of shrubs can also limit the extent of any fire damage. It may be wise to consult your local fire service if the intended shrubland sits adjacent to potentially vulnerable properties or infrastructure, including railway lines and highways.

Existing biodiversity value: It's important to audit the biodiversity value of your site before you consider creating a Shrike Shrubland. You should aim to pick a site with limited existing wildlife value. If your site is already designated, or recognised, for its existing wildlife value, it may well not be a suitable site to create a Shrike Shrubland. If legally designated for wildlife, consult your local statutory nature conservation agency.

If locally recognised as being of value for wildlife, consult your County Wildlife Trust.

2.2 Starting land use

The current use and history of the plot of land you're planning to turn into a shrubland will influence short-term interventions, on-going management, and long-term habitat development. Let's look briefly at existing uses.

Existing Grassland: does the site have existing botanical value? Is it species-rich grassland? If the site is agricultural grassland that has been intensively managed in the past, it's unlikely to have much value. If the site is amenity grassland within a town or village, the situation can be less predictable. It may have escaped artificial fertilisers, and although regular mowing would prevent flowering plants from blooming, they may still be present in the sward. Some urban amenity grasslands are very old and very rich. Not just grasses and wildflowers, but also scarce lichens and mosses. Are there open-habitat species such as Curlew or Lapwing? Are there notable invertebrates associated with, say, open, sunny seepages?

Arable: arable fields often support the last surviving remnant populations of once widespread annual plants ('arable weeds'). These may not be obvious if they're holding on in the seed bank. They may reveal themselves if an arable field is allowed to 'tumble down' as fallow in the early months of shrubland creation. If the site in question supports populations of rarer annual wildflowers, it will probably be best managing it as low input cereals or cultivated fallow. More widespread annual wildflowers can be accommodated within disturbed areas that are integral to Shrike Shrublands

Forestry: many plantation forests were established at a time when the countryside was still of extremely high wildlife value, before agricultural intensification really set in. As such, many plantations were inevitably established on areas of existing wildlife value. Because soil and landform disturbance were often fairly modest, such sites may well retain both the landform and some of the wildlife of the habitats they were established on. Habitats include ancient woodland, heathland and species-rich grassland.

Forestry plantations often offer unusually good opportunities for woodland or open habitat restoration.

Brownfield: If the site was previously developed it could well have considerable existing biodiversity value, and it would be wise to consult your local Wildlife Trust, Biological Records Centre and national organisations Buglife and the Bumblebee Conservation Trust. Some nationally important invertebrate sites are long-abandoned, previously developed 'waste ground'. The site may already be known to be of value; or it may not have been visited but has all the ingredients of a good invertebrate site.

Archaeology: Surface or sub-surface archaeological remains could receive added protection (if, for example, arable land is reverted to grassland), but could also be damaged (if a clump of shrubs is established on such remains, or if sub-surface drainage is 'broken out' across such remains). Seeking the advice of a County Council or local university archaeologist may be wise.

2.3 Some early interventions

Below, we'll consider some early steps you might take to set your site up. You'll find a menu of interventions, some or all of which might be appropriate for you. Your aim is to set the site up in a way that provides a template for diverse plant and animal communities to develop.

This may require no initial work at all - just stand back and enjoy as species recolonisation under their own steam. But if the site has been improved for agriculture, or used fairly intensively, some early interventions can greatly improve how nature re-assembles itself.

Below, I highlight a few measures you should consider.

Reducing nutrient levels: Very fertile soil is the last thing rich communities of grasses and wildflowers need. You really need to take action to reduce nutrient levels as far as possible if they are elevated to an extent by past land-use.

If the land is arable, and soil sampling indicates that it is very fertile, unfertilised arable crops could be sown in the spring and harvested in autumn, with a stubble left over winter, and a further spring crop sown and harvested the following year. Do not fertilise crops at all: the idea is that the crops will soak up nutrients from the soil. These are, effectively, sacrificial crops whose sole purpose is to consume soil nutrients as much as possible.

If you're dealing with existing agricultural pasture, one option would be to close the site up for the summer, and harvest a hay crop in mid-July, when the grass is still green. Remove all the hay cuttings. Harvesting when the grass is still green will help to export nutrients away from the site. It would probably be beneficial to take several hay crops each year, one in, say, May, as long as ground nesting birds such as Skylark and Meadow Pipit aren't present, another in late July. Repeating this process over two or three years can only improve the results in the long-term. Remember, the richest diversity of grasses and wildflowers are found on infertile, not fertile, soils. Fertile soils simply favour the most nutrient hungry species, and these are few in number and very aggressive, outcompeting everything else.

Delay any other intervention until this has been completed.

Re-wetting: The countryside, even what one might at first glance consider to be 'dry land', well away from streams and rivers, more than likely contained wet features - flushes and seepages - that were removed as part of the agricultural improvement process. I cannot stress enough just how common such features once were, and how much inadvertent damage has been done by their removal.

If the site has been under-drained, one should consider making efforts to reverse the effects of that drainage. In-field under-drainage should be blocked or removed entirely. Side drains at field edges should be dammed using soil and/or woody debris. If there is sufficient tree cover around the site, and streams within and around it, it goes without saying that you should seriously consider including Beaver re-introduction within your project.

Why attempt to reinstate lost seepages? Because small-scale and seasonal moisture heterogeneity - wet spots interspersed amongst drier spots - can be key to supporting the varied life stage requirements of many invertebrates. Moisture heterogeneity will in turn support plant species diversity. And birds like Snipe will often visit wetter patches within otherwise dry fields on passage and in winter to feed.

Patches of moisture, especially if they are fed by springs into the summer, can persist even in droughts. Plants such as Meadowsweet and Ragged Robin may well appear within the sward in such damp spots.

Micro-landform: Landform at a tiny scale is usually extremely varied within natural habitats. This varied micro-topography is the template upon which so much diversity of species and communities develops.

If your site has been used for farming, often some of these intricate landforms will have been removed. Arable farmland will have been cleared initially, its surface levelled to some extent, with on-going ploughing further simplifying small-scale landform.

If the site is currently grassland, it may well have been ploughed, under-drained and re-seeded. And bulldozers may have been used in the distant past to remove infield hollows and hillocks.

If, on the other hand, your site is previously developed brownfield, a variety of landforms could already be present. Equally, if the site is covered in plantation forestry, relictual landform may well have survived.

More varied microtopography will result in a more intricate mosaic of habitats.

How can one put back a varied micro-topography? Initially, mechanically!

Ultimately, wild animals will create their own variety too.

Don't forget to consult your local County Archaeologist as appropriate before doing any land-forming. You might even need planning permission, in which case check with the local development control team in your council.

Use diggers to shallowly scrap off and pile up topsoil, creating sunny banks of friable soil. The bare exposed subsoil will provide the perfect substrate for the development of drought-loving plant and animal communities. Fertile soil is the enemy of high-quality shrublands. The sunny side of low banks will be colonised by whole communities of burrowing invertebrates.

Dig hollows of varied depth and extent. Some will be wet over winter into spring and then dry out, potentially being colonised by interesting wetland annual plants.

Others will hopefully hold water over the summer. Scattered clean-water pools - temporary or permanent - are a crucial element of the best Shrike Shrublands.

Mark out scattered cultivated plots: Mark-out areas you intend to cultivate if cultivated plots are to be part of your shrubland. Leave these areas free from other interventions because you'll be cultivating them every few years.

Scattered areas of disturbed ground are an enormously valuable habitat. Historically, Wild Boar would have been a key ecosystem engineer, creating disturbed plots via their rootling behaviour. Extinct wild cattle and wild horses would also have created forms of disturbance, but these would have been qualitatively different.

Wild Boar is very much a neglected native species in UK conservation. Hopefully, we will develop a recovery plan for this species. In the meantime, it's likely to be absent from your site.

It might be appropriate to include domesticated pigs as a short-term substitute for Wild Boar.

Creating brash piles to encourage Rabbits (see below) will introduce a degree of disturbance of great value.

Otherwise, marking out areas that will be cultivated infrequently can act as a substitute.

Plots of a metre or two up to about 10 m² would be ideal. The size of these plots will partly depend on the size of your site. Lots of widely scattered smaller plots are probably more valuable than one or two much larger plots.

Have quite a few amounting to, say, 10% of the site. This is a guess.

Aim to cultivate each plot on a varied timescale. Cultivate some annually, others every three or four years, some every five to eight years. Again, this is really guesswork. You're just trying to create a varied longevity of disturbance. This promotes varied successional stages, each of which will support different wildlife.

I'll leave this by restating that Wild Boar would do exactly this job much better than we can. So, getting them back is, ultimately, essential.

Create brash piles: Brash piles are an excellent hack for Shrike Shrubland creators.

If you're faced with a very open grassland or arable site, creating widely scattered piles of brash can really speed-up the nature recovery process.

A brash pile can be comprised both brash and larger logs. They serve several purposes.

Although Rabbits aren't a native species, they are recognised as a valuable 'ecosystem engineer'. The small pockets of disturbance they create provide shifting opportunities for annual wildflowers to maintain a foothold. Many invertebrates need annual wildflowers, and many need disturbed ground. Rabbits also create the grazed lawns - short turf patches - where Red-backed Shrikes love to capture beetles.

Rabbits drawn to brash piles often initiate new warrens within them, creating small loci of disturbed ground and shorts swards surrounding a brash pile on which a shrike can site and scan.

Brash piles can also attract Song Thrushes, Blackbirds and other dispersers of seed, enabling tree and shrub colonisation and germination.

Reptiles, such as Adders, will frequently bask next to piles of brash and find refuge within them when disturbed.

Dead vegetation, including dead wood from larger branches and logs, support a rich array of wildlife.

Plant introductions to overcome dispersal limitation: Excuse the rather geeky terminology: what this essentially means is that many plants face constraints on their ability both to reach a site and to establish themselves if and once they arrive.

Dispersal and establishment limitation are the main reasons why so many woodland creation projects rely on tree planting (although planting on these grounds often isn't justified, and other, less convincing justifications for tree planting are often invoked!)

The capacity of plants to appear at your site partly depends on its history of use, its current land cover (e.g., bare arable versus thick agricultural sward), its proximity to populations of plants, seed and seedling predation rates, and the presence, or absence, of means of dispersal (e.g., seed-dispersing animals).

Below, I first consider trees and shrubs, after which I'll consider herbaceous grasses and wildflowers.

Introducing islands of shrubs: densely planting whips of trees and shrubs across the whole site will *not* create the kind of habitat that is the focus of this book. Although such planting has its place, I urge you not to do this if you're aiming to create species-rich grassland shrubland mosaics in the early years.

Planting *widely dispersed groups* of trees and shrubs is, though, a valuable intervention to address both dispersal limitation and establishment limitation. It is also a good way of speeding up the process of shrubland development.

Foresters worry about high mortality rates of planted whips, and so justify dense whip planting as a way of mitigating that problem. People aiming to create Shrike Shrublands either as a permanent, open habitat, or as a habitat that will go on to develop as woodland or wood pasture, need not concern themselves too much with moderate mortality rates, if everything dies, you'll need to replant of course. A very common cause of such a failure is that the route mass is exposed to the wind just before planting. Ensure roots are kept moist and away from drying breeze and sunlight and water in copiously during planting.

If your site is directly adjacent to a patch of native woodland, you probably don't need to plant anything. Similarly, if it's surrounded by hedgerows with both trees and shrubs, allowing natural colonisation should be the preferred approach.

If you plan to plant, you should aim to establish widely scattered islands of mixed shrubs and trees species. Plant small nursery transplants (whips) rather than larger specimens. These tend to have higher success rates than older, standard trees. That said, there is something to be said for planting one or two Crab Apple standards within a site. This species provides two excellent keystone resources - blossom and fruits - much appreciated by invertebrates, birds, and mammals.

The species planted will depend on site characteristics, the region you're in, and the composition of local tree and shrub communities. There is plenty of guidance online, and your local Wildlife Trust should be well placed to offer suggestions. The Woodland Trust produces decent guidelines on this too. On the off-chance that Red-backed Shrike does recolonise, include shrubs that they favour. That includes Field and Dog Rose, Hawthorn, Blackthorn, Crab Apple, Bramble etc.

If your site has or is visited by wild or domestic grazers and browsers, you should consider protecting planted trees and shrubs. Rather than encasing each whip within a plastic tube, consider creating fenced exclosures. These are designed to exclude larger grazers and browsers. They are temporary and can be removed once the planted whips have formed an island thicket.

How far apart should your clumps of planted trees and shrubs be? This partly depends on what your long-term objective is. But I suggest spacing each clump of trees and shrubs every, say, 10 to 15 m. Don't plant each clump as a regular grid: vary the spacing.

You can afford to plant whips close together within these clumps. It would be well worth trimming whips down to ensure there is a reasonable balance between root mass and twig mass. This helps establishment.

Introducing herbaceous flowering plants: Basically, we need to get lots of flowering plants established in our open areas of grassland as quickly as possible. A wildflower-poor grassland-shrubland mosaic will be of limited value.

It can take decades for appreciable populations of flowering plants to colonise a site naturally. That slow pace is fair enough if we have time to kill and are relaxed about the rate of nature recovery. In my opinion, we should avoid importing purchased seed and attempt to source material as close to the site as possible. We are really only now discovering local adaptations in plant communities.

But nature is so depleted by us that really we need to intervene to speed up its recovery. And some barriers to colonisation of your site will be entirely human imposed and probably insurmountable for many species.

The invertebrates that need a variety of flowering plants throughout the year for their survival cannot wait a few decades for them to appear. Higher trophic levels of animals will begin to assemble if diverse and rich flowering plant communities are present. Invertebrate biomass will, generally speaking, be increased by diverse flowering plant communities.

Some sites may have wildflowers already present on site or around its edges. These at least have some chance of colonising and expanding within the site. But the presence - or rapid development - of a thick sward of grasses can present a formidable barrier to flowering plant colonisation.

Sourcing wildflower seed to plant. Whether you're starting with grassland or arable, you'll need to find a donor site or sites that support the species of wildflower you want to see within your shrubland. You'll be collecting green hay and seeds from this donor site in late summer. The closer it is to your shrubland creation site, the better.

Try to match the donor site conditions to the receiving site conditions. If your shrubland creation site is on chalk, find a nearby donor site that's chalk grassland, for example.

You need to make sure you don't harm the donor site. If it's an SSSI, you MUST consult the statutory nature conservation agency (e.g., Natural England) as well as the landowner. If it's a County Wildlife Site, consult your local Wildlife Trust. If you're unsure, consult both as a precaution.

You'll probably want to talk to the Wildlife Trust to identify potential donor sites and their owners in the first place.

Only harvest seed from a given donor site or part of the site once in three years. This helps to avoid any harm from over-harvesting.

Harvesting donor hay/seed. The key here is to harvest hay/seed at the donor site just as seed is being set. If the volume of material needed is large, a tractor-mounted forage harvester is best. A strimmer can be used to cut a smaller volume of hay. Apparently, if the hay is slightly moist this can help seed to stick to it. But don't leave your cut hay in piles for any length of time. Get material from the donor to receiving site as quickly as possible. Piles of cut hay can heat up rapidly, potentially damaging seed and reducing germination rates. Plantlife recommends that the operation of cutting, transport and spreading of donor material be completed within half a day.

Sowing/spreading. You need to break up the sward. Ideally, you'll have created cultivated plots within the wider grassland. These plots, which are additional to those to be cultivated every few years, will be the focus for creating areas that are species-rich in wildflowers, from which they can subsequently spread more widely across the site. Spread the hay very thinly, avoiding piles.

To ensure seed has contact with bare soil, roll or stamp it in, or put cattle on. Their hooves will push hay and seed into the soil surface.

Growing and planting wildflower plugs. You should consider growing on seedlings of a few common flowering species to then plant out into established grassland. This can be an effective way of getting over establishment constraints. It complements spreading green hay onto disturbed areas. It's more time-consuming but can be highly effective. You might even involve local schools in collecting seed and growing them on.

Immediate aftercare: The key here is to ensure that germinating seeds and planted plugs aren't immediately overwhelmed by existing, potentially more competitive grasses. If you've sown seed or spread hay into small, scattered patches, you might strim and rake off to keep the sward very short and open. You can also put on cattle or ponies in the early autumn to graze off the sward. Avoid significant poaching.

Arable is an easier starting point. Bare arable land provides a bare template without the competitive grasses that can prevent wildflowers establishing themselves in improved grass swards.

If the arable soil is rich of Phosphates and Nitrates, probably the best initial step is to sow unfertilised spring cereals for a couple of seasons. These hungry crops will deplete the nutrients at least. Phosphate removal is far harder and probably not worth even trying. It will gradually deplete over decades or longer.

Stripping away excess nutrients using arable cropping will set the soil up for wildflower establishment.

Once your arable site is ready, you can deploy the techniques already described in combination to inoculate it with wildflowers.

Don't bother with a commercial wildflower seed mix! These are extremely expensive and unnecessary.

As with the grassland example already discussed above, spread green hay in relatively small patches rather than across the whole site.

Management of an arable site during the year following initial establishment: The year after green hay has been spread, germinated wildflowers will establish themselves but, being perennials, few will flower. They'll do so each spring and summer thereafter.

If the soil is more productive and sward starting to grow on in that first late winter/spring, put on a few cattle or ponies to reduce the biomass. This will reduce competition and help the wildflowers get established. Shut-up the site by remove stock from April to July for the first summer or two.

Afforested sites: In parts of Europe, Red-backed Shrike numbers have increased within plantation forestry clearfells relative to wider farmland. The last few pairs of this species were found on afforested and more open heathlands on sites in the Suffolk Sandlings and the New Forest. More recently, nesting attempts have taken place on lower upland shrubby heath sites on Dartmoor and elsewhere. It's not clear whether such habitat is favoured by the species, or simply represents suboptimal habitat that nonetheless has been less intensively managed than the wider farmed countryside and so held on to shrikes a bit longer. I suspect the latter. Recent successful breeding attempts on

Dartmoor may simply indicate how hostile the wider countryside has become.

If your site is a non-native pine plantation, you can usually simply leave it following harvesting. Quite often such sites are on poor, sandy soils and the ground surface hasn't been seriously altered prior to planting. It may well contain a buried seed-bank of typical acid grassland, heathland or chalk-heath species.

3 Three stylised examples

Having described some of the components of a high-quality Shrike Shrubland and the kind of interventions you might consider in creating one, I'll now give three contextual examples.

The first involves an arable reversion site on a few hectares or acres of lowland chalk. The aim in this example is to create a long-lasting, open Shrike Shrubland.

The second example is a block of improved pasture. It's probably been drained and re-seeded in the past and received regular inputs of nitrogen fertiliser. Again, we're aiming to maintain open shrubland in the longer term.

The third example is on neutral soils next to an existing Oak woodland, where the aim is to expand the woodland and, in the early years, entice some specialist dappled sun loving butterflies to expand into the early successional habitat from coppice and rides maintained for them in the woodland itself.

3.1 Arable field on chalk

Let's assume for this chalk arable example that the site is very open, free-draining and sunny, and the intention is to maintain an open shrubby grassland mosaic in the long term through conservation management.

You're aiming ultimately to create grassland that is both rich in flowering plants characteristic of old chalk grassland, and therefore pollen and nectar, but also more structurally complex than is often the case with open chalk grassland. So, you want taller areas of grassland, tussocks, interspersed with more tightly grazed flowering lawns, and areas of bare recently disturbed ground.

Unevenly distributed within that open, flower-rich grassland will be small pockets of shrubs and a few larger, thicker areas of shrubs, with scattered tall shrubs and trees in some of those clumps.

Context: Paradoxically, a site where there's no existing vegetation, such as an arable field, probably represents the easiest starting point for the creation of a Shrike Shrubland.

The bare ground of arable provides a clean slate for colonisation, with fewer constraints. Whereas an established sward of grasses represents a difficult place for wildflowers to colonise, with lots of competition from grasses and few spots in which new seedlings can germinate, bare ground is largely free of competition and that's just what many seedlings need. You need to make the most of this situation quickly, because some highly competitive species can rapidly colonise and outcompete the herbaceous wildflowers you want to establish.

Initial considerations: Does the site contain any subsurface or surface archaeological features?

Are there any scarce annual wildflowers associated with arable fields present? These can often be present in the seed bank, and sometimes most abundant in field margins.

Is the site under drained? Are there drains around the field edge?

Early interventions: Block or remove any boundary and subsurface drainage.

Create scattered brash piles.

Excavate shallow pools of varying depths and create mounds and friable cliff faces with the arisings.

Scrape off the topsoil in some areas to reveal the chalk subsoil below. Create networks of banks with the arisings.

Locate nearby old chalk grassland sites. Get permission to collect seeds or hay from them.

Identify several areas of a few square metres to focus the introduction of wildflower seed.

Prepare a fine seedbed across these areas to be inoculated.

Brash harvest seed from species-rich donor sites in late summer. Broadcast the seed quickly; this can be done from around mid-August into September.

Plant up and fence scattered patches of native shrubs such as Dog Wood, Wayfaring Tree, Blackthorn and Field Rose.

Subsequent management: Facilitate very light, year-round, or occasional grazing by cattle free from anti-parasitic drugs.

Consider using a flail or volunteer group to very occasionally coppice areas of shrubs, in late January or February the aim being to maintain a mosaic of variable age shrub clamps. Doing this in late winter will give Wildlife time to consume all available seeds and berries.

Long-term development: In this example your aim is to maintain a species rich mosaic of open grassland with scattered shrubs. The brash piles and shrub clamps will, with any luck, draw in Rabbits. These will help to maintain shorter grazed lawns set within longer areas of flowering grassland.

In the short term, the herbaceous vegetation will be dominated by commoner wildflowers. But, given time, usually a few decades, scarcer wildflowers characteristic of older chalk grassland should begin to appear.

3.2 Improved pasture and amenity grassland

Context: Much of the lowland agricultural grassland we see on UK farmland would have been rich in wildflowers if it was grassland prior to the advent of chemical fertilisers. Many have been ploughed and re-seeded, fertilised and managed such that flowering plants are now few if present at all.

This loss of species-rich grassland is a major cause of farmland biodiversity loss. Creating a species-rich grassy shrubland on existing improved pasture is a great way to help nature recover on farmland.

Managed amenity grassland in towns and villages is generally rather bleak as far as wildlife is concerned but will likely have escaped heavy fertiliser inputs.

Re-establishing wildflowers within improved grassland can be challenging. The thick sward of grasses will be a difficult place for wildflowers to establish themselves compared to bare arable. You'll need to introduce a bit of sward disturbance to provide spots where the seeds can easily find contact with soil and germinate free from too much competition from the grasses.

Initial considerations: Select a species-poor site that's not too fertile and has an open, sunny aspect.

Early interventions: If the grasses are vigorous and the site fertile, harvest several unfertilised hay crops, at least once and ideally several times, during the initial couple of summers. Crucially, remove cut hay off site: don't allow cut material to decay on site as this simply returns nutrients to the soil. You're aiming to strip excess fertility and thereby favour wildflowers over more competitive agricultural grasses.

Consider reversing the effects of any sub-surface under-drainage and field edge drains.

Create brash piles scattered widely across the site.

Plant islands of native shrubs with a few trees, within fenced exclosures.

Consider scraping off areas of topsoil to reveal less fertile sub-soil, as long as there aren't archaeological remains that might be damaged.

Excavate scattered clean water pools; these should be a mix of seasonally and permanently wet.

Select a few 3-4m square areas where you'll introduce wildflowers. Strip these of grass and lightly cultivate to form a fine seed bed. Broadcast locally collected seed and spread green hay in late summer-early autumn. Wildflowers in these inoculated patches will gradually colonise more widely. If time and resources allow, enlarge the areas to be seeded as much as possible. If soil conditions are right, try to get and broadcast fresh Yellow Rattle seed. This species is parasitic on grasses and helps to reduce their vigour and competitive ability. This will favour wildflowers.

Consider setting up a small wildflower nursery at which you can grow small plugs of appropriate wildflower species for subsequent planting. Planting plugs in autumn can be a highly effective, if very labour intensive, way to get wildflowers established within permanent grassland.

Create small (a few square metre), lightly cultivated plots. Re-cultivate one or two annually, returning to cultivate a given plot every 1-3 years and longer for some. Maintain these as small plots of disturbance in the long-term.

Subsequent management: Lightly graze the site with cattle free from antiparasitic chemicals.

If possible, continue to import and spread green hay in mid to late July each year for, say, 3 to 4 years after initial establishment.

Continue to cultivate small plots on a varied rotation.

Long-term development: If you want your shrubland to remain open for sun-loving wildlife and grazing animals, ensure summer grazing pressure is very low. Invertebrates will benefit from chemical-free livestock dung in summer but you need to ensure that wildflowers can bloom and set seed profusely. With light cattle grazing, but no specific management of shrubby areas, the site would probably develop as enormously valuable wood pasture over a few decades.

3.3 Woodlands edge

Context: In this example we're aiming to maximise the potential for early successional woodland-associated species in a woodland expansion project. Here, we'll aim to optimise the early years for open habitat specialists while still delivering the longer-term objective of creating closed-canopy woodland, coppice, or more open wood pasture. We'll expand and link up two blocks of woodland separated by an open field of improved pasture or arable.

Rather than plant densely with whips, we'll facilitate the development of a more open, early successional grassland-shrubland habitat mosaic that will persist for, say, the first decade before closing up and moving towards woodland.

Also, an attempt is made to create conditions that might enable colonisation, all-be-it temporarily, by 'woodland' butterflies already present here.

Small, mixed-species groups of a few native tree and shrub seedlings are established using seedlings and seeds collected locally as well as, but in preference to, imported whips.

Within and around the edges of these shrub clumps, early action is taken to introduce native woodland edge flowering plant species, including the food plants of woodland specialist butterflies.

The open, sunny but sheltered conditions may draw them in from nearby woodland rides and glades. The caterpillar food plants you can consider introducing can be determined once you know which species are present in adjacent or nearby woodland and what they require. Butterfly Conservation provides guidance on food plants on its website.

Initial considerations: Ideally, select a strip along the sunny edge of the woodland block. Don't worry too much about deer density: they sculpt rather than scupper shrubland development.

Early interventions: Reverse any under-drainage and side drainage. Many lowland woodlands have been drained in the past, with surface ditches a common feature. This practice has dried out many of our woodlands relative to natural conditions. This may well have contributed to the decline of some woodland bird species.

Existing woodland should be rewetted, and newly created woodlands be set up to ensure a more natural hydrology.

Excavate a series of clean water pools and hollows. These will be sunny in the first decade or two and become increasingly shady through time. The wildlife communities using them will change accordingly.

Create widely scattered brash piles.

Plant groups of native trees and shrubs. Fence these if needed to exclude browsing animals. Consider using wattles or hurdles if they're available from nearby coppicing. Plant appropriate butterfly and moth caterpillar food plants within and at the edges of these clumps.

Subsequent management: Of course, one could manage this woodland edge Shrike Shrubland as a permanent open coppice-like mosaic if an aim is to maintain habitat for associated butterflies. Or it could be nudged towards open wood pasture with appropriate cattle grazing.

Alternatively, you can stand back and allow natural succession to proceed towards closed-canopy woodland.

Long-term development: With this example, the long-term aim is to enlarge and reconnect an area of woodland. Therefore, the site would be allowed to develop into close canopy woodland, coppice, or more open wood pasture. If close canopy woodland was the intention, one could acquire further land on its outer edge to create another block of shrubland, thereby gradually expanding the woodland outwards through time.

If, on the other hand, the intention is to maintain the area as more open habitat for woodland interior butterflies, a coppicing regime could be investigated. The exact prescription for this will depend on local circumstances.

4. Managing Shrike Shrublands

We've briefly considered longer term management in the immediately preceding sections. To recap, in your mind's eye, how would you like your shrubland to look in, say, 30 years? Are you aiming to develop woodland or wood pasture, or would you like to maintain it as an early-successional grassland shrubland mosaic?

If you're aiming at kicking-off the development of closed-canopy woodland, you can stand back after a few years having done the early groundwork described in previous chapters.

The site will move through its shrubland phase to a more closed thicket woodland stage. Trees and shrubs will colonise open areas from the planted islands and adjacent woodland and, after a few decades, you'll have a young, structurally-complex, biodiverse native woodland that'll accumulate an ever changing community of wildlife through time.

To achieve this, you'll need to be careful with the level of cattle grazing, a feature of management that is important for younger shrublands.

British woodlands once had herds of Aurochs (wild cattle) living within and moving through them, but much of the country was woodland, shrubland and wood pasture back then and these wild herds were free to move unimpeded across vast regions rather than being confined to small areas.

I cannot stress enough how important it is to ensure that cattle entering the shrubland are free from toxic antiparasitic chemicals. Dung is a hugely important habitat for a wide variety of invertebrates. Red-backed Shrikes may struggle to raise a brood in a shrubland without dung-associated beetles.

If rather than closed-canopy woodland, you're aiming to develop wood pasture, with, ultimately, scattered 'veteran' trees set with a shrubby 'parkland' with flower-rich, grazed lawns, you can afford slightly heavier grazing and browsing. It's not possible to prescribe stocking rates. They should be determined on a site-by-site basis and will probably require a degree of experimentation.

Any existing woodlands adjacent to your shrubland will very likely support both native and non-native deer. I don't consider even relatively high densities of deer to be as big a problem as others claim, but adding cattle *could* result in cumulative grazing and browsing pressure that's too high for woodland development. You'll have to use your judgement when deciding what if any browsing livestock to allow to enter the site in the longer term.

If you'd like to maintain the site as an open, early successional grassland-shrubland mosaic longer-term, you might combine cattle grazing and browsing with occasional volunteer 'scrub bashing' weekends or mechanical interventions to knock-back shrubby areas on a long rotational basis. Cut a different shrub mound during each operation, cutting each on, say, a ten-year rotation.

This sort of intervention may sound dramatic and destructive. But we once had Aurochs, Rhinos and Elephants crashing through UK shrublands. You're merely replicating ecosystem engineering and processes lost because humans drove European species of megafauna to extinction. Do this in late winter only.

Wild Boar is a key species and should be welcomed across its native range in the UK. Sadly, it's essentially ecologically extinct in the British countryside. Its rooting behaviour certainly looks dramatic and could be said to damage some anthropogenic habitats such as closed-sward, species-rich grassland. But, if present, the disturbance it generates should be welcomed within new shrublands.

Rabbits, although not native, create modest levels of ground disturbance that many plants and invertebrates depend on. The closely grazed lawns they create are used by many birds - not least Red-backed Shrikes - for hunting. Rabbits should be welcomed. Moles are another neglected native species whose hills provide little patches of disturbance that should be welcomed.

5. Discussion and conclusions

Hopefully this short book has inspired you to create, or encourage the creation of, Shrike Shrublands.

We could be creating hundreds of hectares of shrublands annually if only we slightly modified our approach to native woodland creation.

But species-rich shrublands deserve to be created in their own right, in addition to in areas intended for woodland creation. That's because mosaics of flowering grassland with scattered shrubs support a huge array of wildlife, including many species of conservation concern and priority.

What's more, grassy shrublands can provide excellent conditions for grazing livestock. This habitat is entirely compatible with wildlife friendly farming.

Hopefully, organisations engaged in the creation of new woodlands will more often than not adopt the shrubland approach set out here.

In a decade or so, if we have a shifting mosaic of emergent shrublands across the British countryside, we might just see the welcome return of the Butcher Bird to its rightful home in the British countryside.

6. Further reading

I'll provide a list of books and reports to read at my website: stevecjones.uk[1]

The JNCC scrub report can be downloaded here: https://hub.jncc.gov.uk/assets/39590874-8927-4c42-b02a-374712caccd6

---

1. http://stevecjones.uk

7. Acknowledgements

Thanks to the Knepp Estate, RSPB and Natural England for the opportunity to investigate the natural history of the Red-backed Shrike and for inspiring this booklet. The Knepp Estate is superb: emulating their efforts more widely, as part of one's farming system or in one's efforts to pursue rewilding and woodland creation through assisted natural regeneration, could be just what Shrikes need to stage a comeback.

8. About the author

Steve Jones has worked in UK and international wildlife conservation for nearly three decades. He can usually be found on the Isle of Wight, or Cornwall, in the northern summer, and somewhere close to the equator once the first frosts form on his van windscreen.

Find out more at his website: stevecjones.uk

If you enjoyed reading this booklet please consider leaving a review on your favourite online retail store website. This helps other people find it. Thank you.

Also by Steve Jones

Shrike Shrublands
Wildlife Watching Around Ventnor, Isle of Wight
Writers in the Wild

Watch for more at Stevecjones.uk.

About the Author

Steve has lived in Ventnor on the Isle of Wight on and off since 1995. An avid 'patch watcher', Steve considers Ventnor to be by far the best bird watching patch he's ever had. He's keen to encourage other bird watchers and naturalists to explore the area.

Read more at Stevecjones.uk.

Printed in Great Britain
by Amazon

Naheed Kausar was born and married in Pakistan but moved to England a long time ago, and where she had four children. She worked as a teaching assistant for a few years and has been working as a volunteer for the past twenty years. When she was young, she wanted to write, but life got in the way. She wrote her first article as a teenager, and it was printed. She wrote a few articles and tips for *Prima, Women's Own, My Weekly,* and *Best Magazine.* She also wrote a few articles and stories which were published in *The Daily Jung,* the oldest Urdu-language newspaper in Pakistan. People, their wisdom, and their words have always inspired her.

This book is in loving memory of my brother, Mirza Ihsan Kahliq, who died very young. A dear brother and a very brave man who inspired the whole family.

Naheed Kausar

THE PRICE OF MY DAUGHTER'S SHOES

AUSTIN MACAULEY PUBLISHERS™
LONDON • CAMBRIDGE • NEW YORK • SHARJAH

Copyright © Naheed Kausar 2024

The right of Naheed Kausar to be identified as author of this work has been asserted by the author in accordance with sections 77 and 78 of the Copyright, Designs and Patents Act 1988.

All rights reserved. No part of this publication may be reproduced, stored in a retrieval system, or transmitted in any form or by any means, electronic, mechanical, photocopying, recording, or otherwise, without the prior permission of the publishers.

Any person who commits any unauthorised act in relation to this publication may be liable to criminal prosecution and civil claims for damages.

This is a work of fiction. Names, characters, businesses, places, events, locales, and incidents are either the products of the author's imagination or used in a fictitious manner. Any resemblance to actual persons, living or dead, or actual events is purely coincidental.

A CIP catalogue record for this title is available from the British Library.

ISBN 9781035859054 (Paperback)
ISBN 9781035859061 (ePub e-book)

www.austinmacauley.com

First Published 2024
Austin Macauley Publishers Ltd®
1 Canada Square
Canary Wharf
London
E14 5AA

I would like to thank my granddaughter, Sana Shafa, who gave me assistance in publishing my book. Also, I thank my daughter, Mahreen, who sent my script to the publishers a few years ago, which is how my writing journey began.

To my grandsons, Essa, Musa, and Yusuf, even though they are too young to help me write a book they always inspire me to the best. My granddaughters, Iqra and Ayanah, two bubbly and beautiful girls, I wish them all the best and the beautiful future ahead. To my teacher, Mary, who read my stories and encouraged me to fulfil my dreams. And finally, thanks to Austin Macauley Publishers for accepting my manuscript.

Synopsis

Ruby is finding it very hard. Life is tough looking after 3 daughters—difficult emotionally and financially. Aliza, Ruby's eldest daughter, is studying her A-levels. She aspires to become a doctor. Aliza is obsessed with shoes and treats herself to a new pair whenever she wants them.

The Price of My Daughter's Shoes

Since her husband died, Ruby is finding it very hard. Life is really tough looking after three daughters on her own; it is very difficult emotionally and financially. Her husband used to have a very good job as an IT consultant. He was working in the city of Manchester, and Ruby was working in a secondary school as an IT teacher.

Her husband used to say, "I am so proud of you changing young peoples' lives, what a good profession you are in."

Life had been fairly happy when they were married for the past twenty years. They were blessed with three beautiful daughters who always amused them. They had a very beautiful house in a nice area. Her husband loved gardening. He worked all week and kept the weekends free for the family so he could spend time with them. The whole family enjoyed gardening, and they redesigned the garden into a little paradise with delightful walkways and colourful roses in every corner. Aliza was Ruby's eldest daughter, and she was studying for her A-levels at college. She wanted to be a doctor and travel to a third world country and help ill children. She was a kind-hearted girl; she was pretty and had great potential.

She was just at the tender age of 18 but was very sensible. She was not like other girls.

It was mid-afternoon when Aliza came home holding, yet again, another shoe box.

"Another pair of shoes?" asked her mum.

Aliza sat down next to her mum and started telling her that there was a big sale on at the store, and people were buying shoes, so I thought that I would buy some as well. "They were red, stylish, trendy, beautiful, and so cheap too."

"Give a girl shoes, and she will conquer the world," she said to her mum.

"So, tell me how much they were?" her mum asked.

"You don't need to know, mummy; I can afford them as I am working at the weekend, and it will all be paid off."

"But you said you are going to study at the weekend, and also there are many bills piling up, and we need every penny," Ruby said.

She realised that her mum was getting upset, so she sat down next to her and said gently, "You always want me to be happy, so I bought them to treat myself, and I bought you your favourite carrot cake as well. Let's make tea and spend some quality time together."

Aliza was obsessed with shoes, and she had always treated herself to a new pair whenever she saw them. At the moment, things are tight financially, so Ruby didn't want her daughter to spend her money like that, especially when every penny is needed. Ruby knew she had to find another job as well as teaching, because, as the only parent, she had the responsibility of the mortgage payments and bills. Finally, Ruby found a weekend assistant manager's job at the local charity shop. Working in a charity shop was a delightful experience. Her manager, Fern, was a really pleasant woman. Fern was humble and generous. Ten volunteers of all ages were working for Fern, and she managed the shop superbly. Ruby and Fern became the best of friends. Fern was older than Ruby, and Ruby would share her problems with Fern because she was a very good listener. Now Ruby had a friend and a job, and she no longer complained about money.

One spring morning, Ruby's youngest daughters (12 and 14) went to school as usual, Aliza went to college, and Ruby went to the school where she taught. Ruby was in the classroom teaching when suddenly a phone call came from the local hospital, and a nurse said, "I am afraid your daughter has had an accident." Ruby quickly told her Head Teacher and then immediately left work and rushed to the hospital. When she arrived, both the doctors and the police were there. They told Ruby that her daughter Aliza was crossing the road when she was hit by a car. The man in the car had driven off and had hit her because he was talking on his mobile phone. Ruby choked back her tears as she stood there watching her beautiful daughter lying there unconscious; machines and tubes were everywhere. Ruby was devastated; she was filled with confusion and anger. Why had this happened to her daughter?

Doctor Grayson told Ruby, "We are doing tests; we don't know yet how bad she is. Both her legs have been very badly injured."

Ruby was terrified and worried for her daughter's survival. All she wanted was to take her pain away and make her feel better, but there was nothing she could do; she felt helpless. Later that day, Doctor Grayson told Ruby that there were no broken bones, but we are not sure about brain damage. We don't know when she will wake up—maybe tomorrow, or next week, or next month, or she never wakes up. We don't know; let's hope it is soon.

Ruby's world started to crumble. "Oh God, please save her," she prayed.

After a week, God listened to her prayers, and Aliza woke up. Each day she was feeling better and better. Aliza was very fortunate that she did not have any serious injuries or brain damage that the doctor had been worried about. Ruby knew she'd been lucky, and it could have been far worse.

Aliza finished her A-levels and went to university. Time was flying by. The last few years had been stressful for the family; winter had been really harsh, and the recession had dragged on right all through it. Ruby realised that bringing up a family and running a home on her own was the most demanding job in the world. Destiny had finally come to a positive conclusion; Aliza passed her exam with very good marks, and she became a doctor. Ruby and her sisters were delighted. Aliza always wanted to go to a third world country to help other children, but her mum was not that keen.

"Why don't you work here? The NHS needs you here," her mum said.

Aliza responded, "I will one day, but I have signed on for two years, so I have to go abroad,"

Two years later, one bright, fresh summer morning, Aliza started cleaning her room and sorting out all the things she didn't need. She gathered some clothes and shoes for the charity shop. There was the red pair of shoes.

"Are you giving them away?" her sister asked.

"Yes, I want somebody to have them and enjoy them; I will buy another pair to treat myself." "Oh, I see," her sister smiled.

The next day, Ruby took the red shoes to the charity shop.

"Oh, what lovely shoes," her manager said admiringly. "They are quite an expensive brand."

"I know; my daughter has expensive taste. So, tell me, what price should we charge for them?"

The manager said to Ruby, "Why don't you tell me what the price of your daughter's shoes should be?" and the manager went into the back to sort out the bags of new donations that were in the storeroom.

Ruby put the shoes on the counter and started sorting out other things. The door opened, and a few customers came in. One lady saw the shoes and said, "Oh, they are gorgeous," and tried to put a shoe on, but it was too small for her. A few other young women and one older woman tried a shoe on but no luck. Ruby was amused when the old woman tried it on. The manager came back and said to Ruby, "I think the price of your daughter's shoes should be at least £19.99." "I couldn't agree more," said Ruby.

Ruby started to get busy serving customers when suddenly the door opened, and she saw Mrs Brown and her young daughter come in. Mrs Brown was a regular customer; she was a very nice, down-to-earth woman known to be kind, and she always had a warm smile.

A few months ago, Mrs Brown had told Ruby that her husband had been diagnosed with cancer, and she was a heart patient. "Our young daughter Lucy, who is 16 years old, is our carer because we have no other family nearby."

Ruby saw Lucy for the first time. She was beautiful but shy and quiet. Ruby noticed something in her eyes—was it sadness, perhaps due to having too much responsibility for her young shoulders? Like the other customers, Lucy noticed the shoes.

"Oh, they are so nice. I have always wanted a pair of red shoes; can I try them on?" she asked.

"Of course, you can," said Ruby as she handed the shoes over. Lucy put them on. They were a perfect fit, just like Cinderella. They looked so beautiful on her feet. The other customers were also admiring her and the beautiful shoes. Then Lucy asked the price.

"£19.99," said Ruby.

"That is a bit much," said her mum.

"But they are so nice, Mum," the girl said.

"I know, Lucy, but we can't afford that," she whispered to her daughter.

The girl silently took the shoes off and put them on the counter and walked further into the shop. Ruby smiled sympathetically; she could see that the girl really liked the shoes.

Still at the counter, Ruby thought quickly and then she put a new price sticker on the shoes. Mrs Brown and Lucy returned to the counter with a few books they had selected, and Ruby started to ring up the prices on the till. Ruby asked Lucy, "Are you buying the shoes?" "No," the girl replied sadly. "They are on sale from tomorrow. I have just put the sale price on them," said Ruby. Mrs Brown turned the shoes over and looked at the price, it was £4.99. "Oh, can we buy them today?" asked Mrs Brown.

"Yes, I am sure that will be okay," said Ruby.

The girl's face lit up; she was extremely happy. She hugged her mum, and then she went over to Ruby and hugged her, saying, "I am so happy, thanks so much. I know there is no sale tomorrow."

The bright smile on Lucy's face and the big hug she received made Ruby's day. Not a bad price for my daughter's shoes, Ruby thought.

Synopsis

Halima was anxiously waiting for her husband, Ahmed. It was past midnight, and there was no sign of him. At that moment, the door opened, and Ahmed came inside, but he was not alone. With him was a young man drenched in rain, and all of his clothes were wet through. Her husband had brought a homeless man from the city.

Homeless

It was Thursday, 12th January; Ahmad finished his work at 11 pm. As he walked along to the car park on his left side to the bus shelter, he always saw homeless people sleeping there with old, dirty blankets and jumpers—everyone was covered in this winter cold nights. He stopped for a minute, feeling sorry for them, and at that moment, his eye caught one person who was sitting there outside in the shelter. He had no blanket; neither did he have a coat. It was raining badly, freezing cold, and he was just wearing jeans and a shirt. The rain was streaming down his face, and he was shivering with cold.

Halima was anxiously waiting for her husband Ahmad; it was past midnight, and there was no sign of him. "Where is he?" she thought worriedly. At that moment, the door opened, and Ahmad came in all wet. But he was not alone; with him was a young man drenched in rain, and all his clothes were wet through. His hair was flattened on his forehead. He looked pale and weak, and it seemed as if he was going to faint any minute.

"Don't say anything; go and get the warm food and a bed ready, please. I invited him to stay with us," Ahmad said. It was the middle of the night; the children were asleep, and it was a very cold night. At this time, she did not want to argue with him. Her husband had brought a homeless person from the city. She could not sleep a wink.

Ahmad and Halima lived in the Northwest with their two children. Amber, 18, was studying at the university, and their son Imran, 15, was preparing for his GCSE. He loved football and wanted to be a footballer in the future. Ahmad was a bus driver and loved his job. Every day he met new people and took them to their destinations. Though it was a stressful job with long hours, when elderly people travelled, he made sure they had a safe and comfortable journey that made his job worthwhile.

Halima was working in a hospital as a nurse. All the patients liked her. It was the kindly way she had. She always had good or sad stories.

Ahmad could always tell by her face whether she had a good or a bad day. She was in a pleasant mood today and was telling Ahmad that a young couple had twins, and they were gorgeous. But the other day she was very upset as a young man had died of cancer. His parents were devastated. These stories were a part of her life, and she tried to help the family as much as she could.

After two days, the homeless was well enough. He said he would come down for breakfast and meet the family. Amber and Imran were meeting him for the first time. Imran was excited to meet him, but their daughter Amber was not so keen. She felt angry and extremely uncomfortable that a homeless man was staying in their house. She had heard so many bad stories about them.

When he finally came down and set foot in the room, their hearts skipped a beat. The young man was wearing their eldest son's favourite shirt and trousers, who died two years ago in a tragic circumstance.

They all stood silent for a moment. "Come on, son, sit down," Halima said tenderly. "Thanks," he said politely and sat next to Imran. Ahmad introduced his family. "Nice to meet you all," he said warmly. Then the homeless man introduced himself, "I am Martin. My parents died when I was young, I left home and stayed with my friends. Then I finished my studies and looked for a job. I had a few jobs here and there, but I could not find a permanent job. Two months ago, I got ill, and my friend left me. My landlord threw me out, and I was on my own. No job, no money. That's how I ended up at the bus shelter. Thanks so much for your help. I will be gone soon when I will get my strength back."

The family noticed that the homeless man, Martin, did not once look up while he was talking. Instead, he was looking down.

Martin, as he told them his name, was tall with thick brown hair and brilliant blue eyes. He had very white skin and that beautiful smile very familiar to their son who was no longer between them.

"Do you like football?" Martin Asked young Imran. "Oh yes, I love football, and Manchester United is my favourite team," Imran replied enthusiastically. "Mine too," Martin smiled. Soon, they started talking to each other—light talk. However, their daughter Amber wasn't happy. She sat back and sipped the tea.

"Whatever story he told, was he telling us the truth?" Amber asked her mum worriedly. Halima held her daughter's hand. "I hope he will tell us more about himself. Don't worry too much. He said he will leave soon." "I hope so," sighed Amber.

Two weeks passed; Martin settled down in their home. Imran and Martin seemed to be very friendly as they both had the same interest in football. Martin also helped Imran with his homework, as Imran always struggled with maths and ICT. Imran was very impressed with his knowledge.

That friendship with Martin and Imran made Amber even more annoyed, and she was angry with her parents as they blindly trusted a homeless man and letting him stay.

So, one day, Amber confronted him. "I'm not happy that you are staying in our home, and I know you are not telling us the truth about yourself!" she said angrily. "And I know why you are here!" "You do?" Martin asked, gazing at her with a slight smile. "I know you are a thief, or maybe a spy from Russia, or maybe a drug dealer, or even worse, a murderer! I know your kind of people," said Amber. "I bet you do!" Martin could not hold in his smile and looked into her big brown eyes. "Do you think I'm that kind of person?" he said calmly. But she continued to talk to him and said, "Whatever the reason you are here for, please don't hurt us. My parents have had a very rough time," she said sadly. "Don't play with their emotions. My parents see you as their own son who died two years ago in a very bad accident. Their wound is still fresh. They are still not over his death yet." Her eyes teared up. He looked at her, how caring she was towards her family. She is much younger than me. Something broke inside him. He gazed at her for a minute and then left the room quietly.

The time had come to leave. Before leaving, he asked Ahmed and Halima for some money. Ahmad and Halima had already decided that when Martin would leave, they would give him some money. But when he asked for more than a thousand, they were stunned. "Thank God the children were not here, especially Amber," Halima thought. Martin read their expression and said, "To reach my destination, I needed that much money." But he never told them where he was going. "Your money will be returned, every single penny.

You must believe and trust me," Martin said.

It was the sincerity in Martin's voice that they wanted to believe him.

It's been a week now since Martin left, and the house was quieter than ever. No cracking jokes. No laughter. Even Amber felt emptiness. Young Imran was the most upset. Martin stayed with them for three months. Ahmad's family went back to their normal life, but somehow Martin always came up in their conversations.

Days went by, and then weeks and months. Whenever the door knocked or phone rang, they were startled. They never heard from him again. He vanished out of their lives. Half the year was gone already. Halima turned the calendar and sighed. "I know you are thinking about Martin," Amber said. "He is not coming back. Technology has been a lifeline for staying in touch with friends and family. But he didn't. He fooled us. How could we have been so foolish as to trust him? Might be he was in trouble?" Halima said worriedly.

It's been almost a year since Martin came into their lives. Now, Halima and Ahmad believed that he was not coming back. Life is like a river; it flows forward, never looking back.

It was wintertime. Halima was making dinner, Ahmed was watching the news, and Amber and Imran were upstairs when the door knocked. "Who could that be?" Ahmed asked as he opened the door. "Ahmed, who's there?" Halima asked.

"It's Martin," Ahmed replied. Halima left everything and ran to the door. Amber and Imran heard and came running. It seemed that everyone in this house was waiting for Martin. Halima hurriedly moved towards him with arms outstretched; behind were Ahmad and Imran. Amber was the only one who stood her ground.

Martin received a very warm welcome, despite what he had done. The woman standing next to him was very impressed. It wasn't the Martin who came last year into their lives, broken, shattered, and weak. Today, Martin looked strong, confident, and handsome, wearing trendy clothes. The woman with him was also wearing an elegant dress, and her handbag was probably a couple of thousand pounds.

"I hope you are all well. I am so very sorry that I came back after so long. I have so much to tell you; I don't know where to start.

I felt deeply embarrassed that I lied to you about my past. I won't lie today. I am Martin Bentley. By the way, this is my mum, Sarah Bentley. My mum and dad had a great property business in Australia. My dad, James Bentley, was very successful, and he had done everything right.

I grew up in Australia, finished my education as an IT consultant. Though my dad wanted me to join the business, I wasn't interested at all. We had a big argument. I left Australia with my two friends, and I came to England, as I always wanted to see England.

We stayed in a hotel. Then, one day when I woke up and reached for the phone, I discovered that my friends had done me over. They took everything—my card, money, and my expensive clothes. I had to leave the hotel, and all day I was wandering around without any food or drink. Emotionally and physically, I was exhausted. In the evening, I sat at that bus shelter where you had found me. That was my luckiest day. Thank you from the bottom of my heart that your kind people helped me in my difficult time. What a great family you are.

When I reached Australia, my father was on a deathbed. He had a massive stroke. My mum was not good either. My father's business was going to collapse. In these circumstances, when things were on top of me, I lost touch, but I never forgot you. You were always in my mind.

Sadly, my dad died, and I joined my dad's business.

I am not a thief nor a spy from Russia," at that moment he looked at Amber. She flushed and averted her eyes.

"Martin told me about you two months ago," his mum spoke for the first time. "He told me that he had met some amazing people in England. I can't thank you enough for looking after my son. You have created something magical inside him. He is a changed person." She opened her bag and took out a black file, putting it on the table, and said, "This is a document of this house; we paid all the money; this house is yours—a present from us. Inside there is the money that Martin took from you."

"What an amazingly generous present!" Imran shouted.

Ahmed stood up and held Martin's shoulders tenderly and spoke, "I am not bothered about the money that you took from us, neither am I happy about these documents. I am really pleased that you came back and kept your promise and helped restore our faith in humanity."

Synopsis

A story of a mother and daughter's love. A daughter who didn't take her mother seriously. When the mother got ill, nobody took her illness seriously because in her 72 years of life, she was complaining about aches and pains.

Mother

It was a damp and cold morning in November in England. Wafa woke up feeling a bit upset but didn't know why. Amara, her youngest sister, had called her from Pakistan and told her that Mum was not feeling well. She just joked because Mother was always like that, with aches and pains everywhere, but her sister had sounded quite worried. "I bet it's nothing; you are worrying too much," Wafa assured her sister.

Thirty years ago, when Wafa came to England with her husband, she was incredibly overwhelmed but happy to see the beautiful country she had heard so much about. Wafa's husband was working in England as a Telecom engineer and had been for a few years.

Wafa's father was in the army, and she was proud of being a soldier's daughter, but she settled in England, although she always loved her country, her family, and culture. That's why she wanted her children to remember their heritage. She always saved money and took her children back home to meet the family every few years.

Wafa told her children that their Nano is not well, but instead of being worried, they started laughing and joking about their Nano. They just remembered how Nano had a big basket of medicine; she had all sorts of tablets in there for headaches, high blood pressure, cough syrups, and massage oils. It was like a little chemist in the basket. The children also remembered how when she ate a tablet, she used to call to us, "Children, I am eating a tablet," she said, "But why are we here?" the children would ask, "If something happened to me, you should be aware of that." All the children were smirking.

"Don't you worry about Nano; she will be fine," her children assured her. "I hope so," she said worriedly.

Nobody took Wafa's mother's illness seriously because in her 72 years of life, she was always complaining about aches and pains, but it was usually nothing serious, and then Mother would take a tablet from her magic basket, and she was fine in a few days. She would not go to the doctor, as Mother didn't trust them.

When Wafa's sister, Amara, rang her a few days later and told her that Mother had been admitted to the hospital, then Wafa realised that Mother is not well, and she is seriously ill. Mother had agreed to go to the hospital, where she had always refused to go. Wafa panicked; she wanted to fly as quickly as possible to be with her mum. She started sobbing and praying at the same time. Fortunately, Wafa and her husband had a plane ticket for the day after tomorrow, but it seemed time was not moving quickly for that day to come.

Her sister, Amara, and her husband came to the airport. Her sister always looked happy and full of life, but today she looked tired, and Wafa sensed disappointment in her tone. They hugged each other, Amara cried; she couldn't control herself either, and she knew that Mother was not well. Upon landing, Wafa went straight to the hospital. Mother was in a special care unit. She was lying straight on the bed, and there were so many wires attached to her. Mother looked exhausted, sick, and she had lost so much weight. Wafa's heart sank. She wanted to cry, but she couldn't; she wanted to scream, but she didn't. Instead, she held her mother's hand, kissed her forehead, and a single tear dropped, but she turned to face the other way. Mother was so glad to see Wafa and her husband. In her week voice, she started talking to them. Wafa sent everyone home and stayed with mother; she didn't want to miss any moment with her.

Memories flooded back about how mother used to cook. One of Mother's passions was cooking. Her chicken kormas, kofta (spicy meatball), and aloo paratha were to die for, and she made many more tasty dishes. The air was filled with delicious aromas that still linger with her today; she was a wonderful cook. Wafa also remembered when mother was making lots of dishes; in this process, she always made so much mess in the kitchen. Wafa did not like that because she had to clean the kitchen. Sometimes, as mother and daughter, they had arguments because they both had different opinions on different matters. During one stormy argument, Wafa said some harsh words and then said to her mother, "You don't know anything."

"And you do," Mother said to her and smiled, looking at her daughter who was growing up so quickly. Wafa remembered when she said that to her mother that she didn't know anything. That evening she felt very embarrassed and ashamed that she had spoken to her mother in that tone. Wafa thought deeply about the mother who held her finger and taught her how to talk and walk. She realised she had said to her mother, "You don't know anything." Despite having many ups and downs with her mother, she loved her, and this realisation brought a regretful tear to her eyes.

Later, when Amara was telling Wafa about Mother going to the hospital, she mentioned that she opened her old box, took out all the money, bank books, and jewellery, and handed them to their father, saying, "I don't think I am coming back home; please forgive me."

Mother was in the hospital for a few days, and Amara put all the kitchen things away in the cupboards. The house was so quiet and felt so empty with Mother in the hospital. The kitchen was tidy because no one was cooking.

Mother was naive and a pure, noble woman. She didn't know what was happening in the world, nor did she know about family politics. She was pretty with very healthy-looking skin, not very tall, and had very little education, but she had a great sense of humour. Wafa's father was a 6-foot tall, charming, strong soldier, and he made Mother look even smaller than she was when they stood together. Mother's priorities had always been her husband and children.

Wafa had lots of her friends who had settled in England and came from Pakistan. They had busy lives and never visited their parents or homeland. However, For Wafa, it was crucial that her children knew their heritage.

Wafa's children regularly visited their homeland, and they would always go to Nano's house. The children would sit for hours, listening to Nano's jokes and stories. Her children adored her and loved the time they spent with her.

Once Mother said to Wafa, "Every time you visit us, it must cost a lot; save your money for your children." Wafa answered, "Something more important than money is spending time with you and making future memories with you." Mother smiled kindly and said, "God bless you." Mother also said, "Your children like my medicine basket; when I am not around, you take my basket for your children."

Mother attended the hospital for what she thought was a very bad stomach upset that wasn't getting better, but it turned out to be more serious. The doctors did more and more tests as time went on, and Wafa was frantic with worry.

The 13th of December was a day that Wafa will never forget. It was a Sunday, and the time was 7 am. Wafa's youngest sister was staying with her mother in the hospital. It was Wafa's brother who took the call that everyone dreaded. Mother, who was suffering from what she thought was a stomach upset, was getting worse. Wafa dashed to the hospital as fast as she could, but by the time she got there, she had already gone. It was horrible. Wafa felt so full of regret. Why had I gone home? Why hadn't I stayed longer?

When your mother dies, nothing is the same again. Life has changed a lot since Mother died.

After four weeks, Wafa came back to England with a heavy heart. Although it is a natural event that everybody has to go through one day, losing your mother doesn't get any easier, she thought.

Wafa brought back Mother's medicine basket along with other things. Her children were delighted to see Nano's basket, and Wafa was honoured that Mother had chosen her to have her basket. There were so many beautiful memories attached to that basket; her eyes filled with tears. Eventually, life went on, and she couldn't bring her mother back, although she took comfort from her memories. She discovered that going back home was the best decision. The children had fond memories of Nano; they always talked about her, what a beautiful, funny person she was.

One bright sunny morning, Wafa and her children were spring cleaning. Her mother's basket was on the top of the shelf, and Wafa said to her son, "Will you get it down; I have to clean it?" But when he picked it up, it slipped from his hand and fell upside down. Wafa saw a thick envelope fall from the basket. She opened the letter and saw the money inside. This was the money that Wafa had given to her mother as a gift when she visited Pakistan, but Mother had never used the money but kept it for Wafa and the children. Tears filled her eyes, and she squeezed her eyelids tight, whispering, "Oh dear Mother."

Synopsis

A professional working woman, Mona, decided to work in a charity shop. After a big tragedy hit her life, she looked sad, frustrated, and lost, as if her world had ended.

The Charity Shop

When she entered the shop, her bracelet caught the door handle, and she nearly tripped over. She quickly regained her balance. Immediately, she noticed that the new volunteers were working near the shelves. One of them saw the incident, and she saw a smirk on his face. She did not like that. She pretended that she didn't see it, and went back, put her bag in the locker, made a cup of tea, and went into the shop. She put a smile on her face and looked around confidently.

Mona had been working in the charity shop for a while now. Before that, she was a professional working woman. But when coronavirus hit the world, her happy life collapsed in a mess of disruption. First, her father was a victim, and then her very loving, caring, intelligent doctor husband caught the virus, and it was fatal. They both died in three months. She was left with elderly women, one her mother and the other her mother-in-law. Both were very fragile and looked up to Mona.

Mona always looked confident and calm doing her full-time job. But what was happening in her mind, nobody knew. She lost her beloved father and dear husband—two men who supported her the most in her life. Emotions boiled and simmered, and one day she collapsed.

Mona resigned from her job and stayed home for one year. She looked so frustrated, sad, and lost, as if her world had ended. Both elderly women saw Mona like this, and it broke their hearts.

One Sunday afternoon teatime, the three women were together, remembering the past. Mostly, that meeting was to tell Mona that whatever happened, life still goes on. You are young, educated woman; don't lose hope. You will find happiness again.

Both women's wisdom and knowledge persuaded Mona to look after herself and find a new purpose in life.

Finally, she found a job in the charity shop, a light, flexible job as a shop assistant closer to home. However, she had always worked in offices with big companies. Mona packed away her laptop and started working with people face to face.

On the first day, her first customer was a young man, who came with a middle-aged woman. He was childish and clumsy, touching everything. Once or twice, he dropped a few things from the shelves. Soon, Mona realised that the woman was his caregiver. He chose a few things and came to the counter, saying nice things about the shop. When Mona gave him the change back, he noticed Mona's bracelet. "Oh, that's beautiful. Can I buy that?" Both women laughed, and he laughed too. At least he's happy, Mona thought. He left, but he lit up Mona's day.

People from all walks of life come to the shop. Mona met some memorable characters that stand out above the others. Sheila was one of them, who inspired her the most. She was a tiny 80-year-old woman. Her husband died when she was 39 year old. She had no children and never married again. She dedicated her life for volunteering. Mona had a special respect in her heart for this tiny, sweet lady. Monday was Mrs Thomas's day; she always came with her husband and son. It must be that her husband can't drive, she thought. Her husband seemed kind and calmer, but her son was not. He stood right behind her mother, kept saying, "You don't need that; you already have this. Why are you taking so long? Come on, Mother, we are so late." Poor Mrs Thomas was panicking. At this point, Mona wished that she could grab him and throw him outside, letting Mrs Thomas shop peacefully. She smiled at her wildest dream.

Mona was enjoying her job more than she ever enjoyed her first job. Every day, meeting knew and interesting people, some remaining mysterious. Most people are an open book; they say what they feel. Mr Mark, when he put a foot in the shop, started blurting out his opinion on everything. Mona didn't know what to say; she just smiled.

Sometimes she even wondered how the charity shop started. Whoever had the idea, it was a wonderful idea. So many people connected with the organisation. People were so generous, giving so many donations, unbelievable. The charity shop was far all communities, especially for the elderly. They can excess many other resources for free. That was remarkable.

The new volunteer was working near the book corner. He was chatting with other customers, but he was putting the books the wrong way round. Mona went to him and said, "Excuse me. Our manager told us to put the books on the shelf with the title of the books showing in front." He responded, "Oh, I see. Thanks for letting me know." Mona put other things correctly and ordered him to clean the shelves as well. He smiled weirdly. Mona didn't like that either.

That afternoon, another incident happened. An old man came with a donation. He had three bags. Mona asked him to leave it there. When she picked up the bag to take it to the backroom, it was so heavy that it ripped from the bottom, and all the bits and bobs scattered on the floor. The shop was full of customers waiting to be served. She was panicking, and at that moment, the new volunteer came running to help. She was so grateful. At the end of the day when he was leaving, he came to the counter, looked straight into her eyes, and said, "It was very interesting meeting you." He smiled and said, "See you soon." This time, Mona noticed his smile was quite charming.

One sunny Wednesday afternoon, a woman came in. She was short, almost dwarfish, with sadness written on her face. Mona was carefully watching her. She picked up a bone china mug and then went to the jewellery corner. From the corner of her eye, Mona saw that she took a necklace and put it in her pocket. When she came to the counter, she only wanted to buy the mug. Even though Mona asked if there was anything else, she said no. There were a few customers behind her, and Mona didn't have the courage to ask her or didn't want to embarrass her in front of other people.

Coincidentally, one day Mona met her in the street. She asked her, "Why did you steal? I saw you put the necklace in your pocket." The woman's eyes filled with sadness. She took the necklace out from her pocket and handed it to Mona, saying, "Take it back; it's not needed anymore. I haven't had the money. I took it for my mum; she was in the hospital. She died two days ago." Mona was speechless.

It was fabulous; the festive season was approaching, and there was a happy buzz in the air. All the volunteers and staff were waiting for the manager's announcement. It was a Christmas tradition to take them out for Christmas dinner. After dinner, the manager gave presents to all the volunteers. It was a big occasion, and all were very excited. Mona was among them.

The manager was waiting for a special guest. Mona was sitting where she could see the front entrance. She saw a reflection of that volunteer who once worked in the shop. He came towards the table, and the manager stood up, and all the others did too, but Mona stayed seated. He wore a black suit with a matching shirt and tie. His hair was neatly set, and he was handsome, Mona thought.

The manager introduced him to other staff and volunteers. "This is Adam Young, our Area Manager." A spoon fell from Mona's hand onto a bone china dinner plate, making a noise. Adam looked at her and laughed gently.

Later, he sat next to Mona as there was an empty seat. "Why didn't you tell me?" Mona said embarrassingly. "I quite enjoyed working as a volunteer under your supervision," he said jokingly. He looked around and then at Mona's face, which was glowing. "I think this evening is going to be so special," she smiled with such cheer she had never felt before.

Synopsis

In life, you meet some people, but right away, you hate them. It was not that she did not know her, but she grew up with her. She was a servant's daughter, who was living in a tiny servant quarter in the corner of the big house.

Heartbeat

She was living the dream: money, beauty, success—she had it all. The daughter of a millionaire, Mr and Mrs Khan's only daughter, Mirah Khan, enjoyed a lavish lifestyle with her father's favouritism evident. Servants, a butler, and a cook surrounded her.

In life, you meet some people whom you immediately dislike. It was not that Mirah did not know her, but she had grown up with her. Zermeena, known as Meena, was a servant's daughter residing in a tiny quarter in the corner of the big house.

Meena had an unusual appearance, with long feet and hands, a small and skinny body, very dark skin, and greasy, curly hair. One look at her made you want to look away. She was a year or two younger than Mirah Khan.

Meena took care of the kitchen, among other servant duties. Despite her unconventional looks, Meena had a good nature. She was warm-hearted, an excellent cook, and looked after Mrs Khan. In fact, she was Mrs Khan's favourite servant. Whatever Mirah said to her, Meena listened with a smile and responded, "Yes, Ma'am."

Mirah Khan was a beautiful young woman. Beauty was her weakness. She always liked beautiful things in life—in her home, wherever she went, beauty impressed her. She couldn't stand ugly people, and if at any moment she saw Meena, her temperature went sky-high. She had a sharp tongue, and whatever was in her mind, she said it loud to poor Meena, who ran away and hid in the kitchen. Only seeing her ruined Mirah's mood for the whole day. If it were up to Mirah Khan, Meena would have sacked her right away, but her father always calmed her down and said, "Look, Meena's ancestors looked after our family. Then their parents were our family servants, and when they died, they said to us, 'Please look after our daughter.' Since then, she has been no trouble to us." But Mirah Khan hated her so much that she always made fun of her, especially when her friends were around. They joked and laughed loudly, and at that moment, Meena ran to the quarter and cried loudly.

That was the only psychological problem with Mirah Khan. In her practical life, she had a busy, widely successful business in catering. She was a bright, intelligent woman, brilliant with her customers and friends. Though not married yet, she worked with her father. He was very pleased with her, and they both had deep love and respect between them.

It was a Saturday chilly night in January when Mirah went out with her friends to the city's top restaurants for her best friend's birthday celebrations. The restaurant was filled with brilliant lights and an exotic blend of spices, making people hungry. The meal was delicious, and they all enjoyed the food and each other's company. It was late and very cold when she walked to the car park. Feeling tired, she opened her car door, felt dizzy, and suddenly experienced a pain in her chest. "I had too much to eat," she thought. Eager to go home, she drove fast, but another wave of pain hit, and she collapsed behind the wheel.

It was a miracle that she survived. After a few days, she woke up. Her mind was still fuzzy, and she was covered with bandages, her body aching. Her parents were at her bedside, but her pain was tremendous. She kept fainting, and her heartbeat kept skipping. Doctors conducted tests, but they couldn't identify the issue. Her parents reassured her that she had a minor accident, but deep down, they knew something serious had happened. Still, they remained optimistic.

The following week, on a gloomy day, doctors finally discovered that Mirah suffered a heart attack, and due to delayed help, her heart was severely damaged.

"Heart attack? Not thirty yet. How could that have happened?" She was young, well, and healthy, but sometimes you don't know what's happening in your body, and heart disease has no boundaries—young and old, children also have heart disease, as the doctor explained. "We are going to operate on her to mend her heart; hopefully she will be fine."

After a month, all her wounds had healed, but her heart remained damaged. Despite two unsuccessful operations, her heart did not respond to the treatment. She fell into a deep depression, realising that everything could change in the blink of an eye. Her life, once carefree, had turned upside down. Looking into the bathroom mirror, she could not recognise herself—she had put on so much weight, lost her beautiful complexion, and her charming, dazzling body had disappeared because of the medication. The beauty she was once proud of had vanished quickly, and life became painful and disempowering. "Even if my parents sell all their property and wealth, they still can't buy a heart for me," she thought.

Desperately in need of a new heart, doctors put her on the urgent transplant list, assuring her that she would be fine after the transplant, God willing. In that moment, she flashed back to a few years earlier when she was in college. One day, she and her friends saw a young man standing over the side giving leaflets to the people. He handed one to Mirah. It was from a heart organisation who was persevering people to sign up as a heart donor and save lives. Mirah and her friends laughed, ripped the leaflet, and threw it in the young man's face, saying, "Do you think we'll give you our heart? No chance." They laughed, joked, and walked away. However, Mirah turned back and looked at the young man's face. How could she ever forget that expressions on the young man's face, it had always stuck in her mind. She was overcome with embarrassment and guilt and realised how wrong she was. Now, she knew the real pain of life.

A few weeks later, suddenly, a ray of hope broke, and then the news came: there was a heart, and it was a match. The doctors were hopeful this time and said, "This will be a lifesaving operation, Insha Allah."

Fifteen hours later, the operation was over, and it was successful. When she woke up, her parents were at her bedside, and the doctors told her, "Soon you will have your life back; the donor came to us just the right time." She was so grateful and wanted to meet the family and thank them, but she noticed that her parents were reluctant to say anything.

After a few weeks, she left the hospital and was well enough, her health was returning, and new plans were made. She asked her parents again about her donor. This time she was very determined to meet the family, feeling gratitude for being alive to all those who helped her, especially the person whose heart now beat in her. Then her parents reluctantly told her, "It was Meena. She was crossing the road and was hit by a speedy car. Her last words were, 'Give my heart to Ma'am Mirah." When she heard that name, thunder roared, and it seemed like a lightning strike had fallen over her.

She stood at Meena's grave with the most expensive bouquet of flowers, her heartbeat rhythm in her chest making a beautiful sound of music, and she spoke to Meena in a good manner for the first time.

"Your kindness has given me hope and my life back. Thank you a million times. I am sorry in a million ways that I hurt you; you were a much better person than me. Please forgive me." Shameful tears rolled down her cheeks.

Synopsis

Nina was angry with the whole world—her happiness snatched away from her when she was six. She was an unpleasant child, rude, badly behaved, and threw tantrums. Whenever some family fostered her, and then they no longer kept her for just two or three weeks, that made her even more bitter.

Lesson Unfolded

What the hell were these oldies doing at this time of the morning? It was only 5:30 am, so dark and freezing; January had just started.

Nina saw all the lights were lit up from the bungalow opposite her council flat. She couldn't resist thinking about them, but then she closed the bathroom door behind her, emptied the can of coke with the big bar of chocolate, and went back to bed.

At 11:00 am, Nina woke up, opened the old dirty curtains, and saw the old couple were ready to go. From their footwear, she guessed they were going for a walk. She felt guilty but then moved from the window, turned the TV on, flickering through the channels. There was nothing good on, so she turned the TV off and wandered around in her tiny, old flat like a lost soul.

Nina moved to this council flat a week ago. Mrs David, a social worker, was very kind to her. She knew the poor girl's history. She had a very rough time. She had once been so happy, blissfully living with her parents, with food on the table, a cosy bed to sleep in, and an adorable baby brother to play with. Laughter and happiness filled the home. She lived in a dream of a happy life. But a freak accident changed everything. Her Mum, Dad, and little brother died on the scene, and she came under the care of social services.

Nina was angry with the whole world, her happiness snatched away from her when she was six. She was an unpleasant child, rude, badly behaved, and threw tantrums. Whenever some family fostered her, they no longer kept her for just two or three weeks, which made her even more bitter.

Time flew by, and she'd grown up now, struggling with self-esteem issues. Nine was the youngest woman at the shelter home, so Mrs David thought she should leave the shelter and live independently and make something of her life.

It'd been two weeks now in her flat. She was lonely, depressed, emotional, and boredom was her biggest problem. She was sitting near the window, looking back at her life.

"Is my life going to be like this forever?"

She asked herself.

The answer was NO.

"So, what do I have to do?" She remembered what Mrs David had said when she handed the key to her council flat, "You are very lucky that you have this flat. I know this is small, old, and dirty, but this is your own place. There are so many women still waiting for the space of their own."

"I know," Nina said thankfully. Mrs David warmly hugged her and said, "Life is to be enjoyed, being happy. It is up to you now what you get out of life. Take care," and then she left.

Later in the evening, Nina made a plan for her future and then went to bed. The next morning, at 5:30 am, the alarm went off. Nina quickly turned the alarm off. "Oh my God, so hard to wake up this early," she mumbled, but then she left the bed. She peeped from her window at the bungalow in front of her. Indeed, they were awake; all the lights were lit up. She went to the bathroom and put cold water on her face; she was fully awake now. "What shall I do now?" she asked herself. She remembered when she was in the shelter, there were women from a cross-section of society, from all over the region. Some had different faiths; older women would wake up in the morning, some would pray, some would read holy books, and some did yoga. But Nina decided to clean her bathroom.

After an hour and a half, her bathroom was sparkling clean and fresh, and she made a list of things she needed for the bathroom.

Time for breakfast; she cooked a bowl of porridge, chopped some fruit and nuts, and started enjoying her proper breakfast for the first time. At eleven sharp, she was ready, fastening her shoelaces, and at that exact time, the old couple came out and started walking towards the right path. Nina started to follow them. They went to the nearest memorial park. The sun was shining, a beautiful smell was in the air, and the council workers were cutting the grass. A few young mothers with their lovely babies were chatting with each other. Nina felt happy overwhelmed. She was enjoying being out in the weather.

After one round, she was breathless. She sat on the bench, catching her breath as the old couple walked past her for the second round. A sense of shame came over her.

For the past four weeks, Nina was waking up with the old couple, walking with them. That routine suited her; she was thinking clearly, feeling energetic, and her spirit was uplifted. She desperately wanted to meet the old couple, who gave her hope and motivation, but she didn't bring up the courage to introduce herself.

One sunny afternoon, Nina was putting her washing out, suddenly caught her eyes on the courier with the parcel knocking on the old couple's door. She knew they were not home; she saw them going out. She dropped everything and run towards the bungalow, speeding like a rocket. With heavy breath, she said to the courier, "I will take that." The courier looked at her with disbelief. "OK, if you say so, thanks," he passed the parcel and put the card in the letterbox.

She held the parcel tight, close to her chest, like a very precious thing.

Finally, the old couple arrived. She saw them from her window, waited a few minutes, but she couldn't wait any longer. She knocked on the door, and the old man came out. "I am Nina," she said cheerily, "Your parcel." She handed the parcel. "I live there," she pointed her finger to her flat. "I moved here four weeks ago." "Oh, nice to meet you. I am Jack, and that's my wife Lynn." She came to the door with the kindest smile on her face. Nina loved them right away. What a fantastic couple, she thought. Lynn invited her in, and Nina was so happy, as she had never been invited to come in. She always wanted to meet the old couple, and Nina accepted the offer happily.

When she entered the bungalow, she was in for a surprise. Though the bungalow was small, they set it up uniquely. There was a corridor leading to a room with two corners, a weird kind of room she had never seen before. In one corner, there was a large fish tank with amazing, colourful fish swimming behind it. There was a big mirror on the wall behind the fish tank. In the other corner, there were the most beautiful and unique birds in their cage, surrounded by a beautiful selection of exotic plants—climbers like big ivy and jasmine, with lots of different flower colours and textures among the big plants.

Behind the wall to her right, there was a big mirror reflecting a sparkling blue sea where fishes were swimming. To her left, a corner transformed into an exotic garden with the prettiest birds flying, humming, and butterflies fluttering—it looked heavenly.

Mr Jack explained, "Fishing is my hobby, and the birds are so special for Lynn, so we wake up early in the morning to feed our hobbies." "Oh, I see," she spoke like she was dreaming, and she had her answer.

The next day, she went to the pet shop and bought some seeds and a bird feeder, hanging it in her small backyard in front of her tiny window where she could sit and watch.

To her amazement, the birds kept coming and eating the seeds. She was so happy to see that. She discovered that the smallest things can give the greatest pleasure, something she never realised before.

Nina kept going to the pet shop; she was so caring and dedicated towards the birds that the pet shop manager offered her a job. Nina was thrilled.

Today, she received her first payment, and she invited the old couple for tea. She was deeply moved by their determination. Even though they were old, they were still enjoying life. Nina learnt that whatever age you are and whatever circumstances you are in, you can have new experiences and new ambitions, and you can rebuild your life again.

Synopsis

In 1960, when young Zara got married, she had a dream like any other girl; a beautiful wedding ceremony and many photographs. However, their wedding plans were rushed, and not a single photograph existed. She was devastated.

The Photograph

In 1960, when Zara got married in the North of Pakistan, it was in a small village. She wasn't expecting her wedding to be like this. She was a young girl, and she had dreams like any other young girl. She wanted lots of flowers, poetry, and music as part of her wedding ceremony and many photographs, and she wanted a nice, tall, handsome husband.

Her last wish was granted; her husband Ali was a very tall, handsome, and a loving person, but her wedding day was not what she had expected. Zara's husband was from England. He had visited Pakistan on a short-term visa. They hadn't much time to prepare for their wedding, and their wedding plans were rushed.

Ali knew that she was not happy about her wedding day; not a single photograph existed, but he said, "We have each other, we will take as many photos as we like when we go back to England," "I know," she said sadly.

One day shortly afterwards when she was busy packing to go England, Ali came home, and he was in a good mood. "Zara, tomorrow, please get ready and wear your wedding dress as we are going to the city. I have booked an appointment with the photographer, and we are going to take a wedding photo." She was delighted to hear this. So, they went and had their photograph taken. The photographer said to come back a week later, and it would be ready.

Zara and Ali were due to leave the following week, and Ali needed to sort out all their documents, including a visa for Zara, their travel tickets, and to make sure everything was ready for their departure. Unfortunately, Ali became ill as he was working so hard and was only just better in time to finalise the documentation and catch the plane back to England.

At the airport, all the relatives came to say goodbye and gave them both a great send-off. On the plane, Zara and Ali settled into their seats for the long journey. The journey and the new dreams could now begin for them. Just two hours before they reached England, Ali remembered that they had left the wedding photograph behind. They had forgotten to pick it up from the city. Zara was devastated.

For Zara, leaving the country and her parents' house was a big life change. She was young, now married, and about to arrive in England. This was an exciting and new but daunting beginning, and not having the wedding photograph made things even harder.

Upon arrival, Zara saw this was a different world with incredible and interesting places to see; clean roads, big buildings, and so many cars. Everything was so amazing although very different from her own country, she thought; the culture was different, and the language was difficult to understand.

A few weeks later, on a grey, gloomy, and cold day, Zara thinks back to her childhood that was filled with love and what she has left behind. Beautiful sun-filled days, clear blue skies, smoke rising from the chimneys of the houses, and the sound of birds singing. The reality for Zara was so different; she was in a strange country and felt so alone and missed her family.

Zara was startled by a knock at the door; it was the postman with a letter from her family. The letter read,

"Dearest daughter,

I hope you are ok and living happily with your husband and that you are settled in your new country. We are all very happy for you. Your sisters and brothers always talk about you, and your mother still calls your name thinking you are in the house. Then she realises you are not here anymore; she laughs, but I can see the tears in her eyes.

Anyway, your mother sent me to the city to buy some medicine for your brother. When I walked along to the medical store, I passed a photographer's studio. I saw a photo hanging upside down. I went in and picked up the photo and looked, and it was you and your husband. I asked the shop assistant why the photo was hanging upside down in the window. He explained, 'When the customer doesn't come back for the photo, it is our policy to put it up to see if anyone recognises the people in the photo so it can be collected.' I asked if I could take the photo as you are my daughter, and I could send it to you. The shop assistant happily agreed.

Be happy, my daughter.
All my love,
Your father."

This made Zara cry and smile at the same time as she now had the photograph of her wedding that she always wanted.